TABLE DECORATION

Stylish Ideas for all your Entertaining
with an introduction by
Michael Smith

ANDREA SPENCER

Macdonald Orbis

Special Photography by Malcolm Robertson

Illustrations by Lucy Su

A Macdonald Orbis BOOK
© Macdonald & Co (Publishers) Ltd 1985, 1987
First published in Great Britain in 1985
by Orbis Publishing Ltd, London

Reprinted in 1987 by
Macdonald & Co (Publishers) Ltd
London & Sydney

A member of BPCC plc

Printed in Italy

ISBN: 0 356 14413 5
Macdonald & Co (Publishers) Ltd
Greater London House
Hampstead Road
London NW1 7QX

CONTENTS

Introduction

I was brought up in a Victorian-cum-Edwardian environment, the last in a family of six children. Although we each had our share of humdrum chores to do, so did we have a compensating 'plum'. Mine was to set the table when guests were expected, for my down-to-earth Yorkshire mother admitted that 'our Michael' had a bit of a flair for it.

The secret of all table settings is the element of surprise, but after that, the *under-plate*. I was no more than eight years old when I made this discovery, though my mother objected to what she saw as extra washing-up. For my part, I could never understand her resistance to using her china — she hoarded dinner and tea services like other people collected stamps. The glowing sunshine hue of one in particular — which I was never actually allowed to lay on the table — regularly comes to mind as I prepare a table in my London home today. Each setting in this magnificent collection had *five* plates with wonderfully coloured borders of blue, green, coral and gold, 'swept' edges and an attendant array of tureens, platters, dishes and ladles.

Whatever happened to the generously proportioned plates of those far-off days, the pudding plate a good 8 inches across, the man-size dinner plates, those glorious soup plates of Olympic proportions? Services like these can lift the presentation of a simple egg mayonnaise from the mundane into the spectacular, especially if the sauce is coloured with the green of chopped herbs or the soft coral of smoked salmon purée. Add a simple twist of cucumber, and then stand the little plate on a larger one; and place that on a larger plate still, with a folded napkin in between. No cooking, no extra expense, but a great sense of style — and only one small plate to wash up!

Now that vast dinner services like these are so rare and so costly (except in the occasional country house sale), my advice is to select a set of eight handsome dinner plates, colour co-ordinating them with your dining room scheme, after which plain white china can be used ad lib. That handsome, nay exotic, plate should be in position when you seat your guests to make the strongest impression. Having made your choice, work around it, with candles and napkins to match. And flowers too, though I prefer to see them arranged in vast tanks in other areas in the room.

Every time I find anything I like, I buy it, trusting in the

'design computer' present in all our minds to take sub-
liminal care of whether it will 'go' or not. Nevertheless,
there are a few simple rules to follow when buying a piece
of china: is it of a *size* you need and will use? A small dish,
for example, which is right for a water ice, can double up to
serve an avocado. Look for even one blob of your chosen
colour. Does the *shape* echo or complement something you
already have? Does it have a related *texture*? And remember that old always works with new, if the answer to any of
these questions is yes.

When I was arranging the elaborate table settings for
Upstairs Downstairs and *The Duchess of Duke Street*, there
would often be up to forty items before each guest . . . a
suite of ten glasses for a start. Today one well-shaped
(tulip) wine glass will suffice; but if there is an occasion on
which you are serving different wines in different glasses,
there is no reason why you should not mix and match as
you would the china. People like odd glasses, and it is
particularly flattering when you can offer them their per-
sonal favourite. And if you have fish eaters, or dessert
knives and forks with pretty handles, use them on the table
to enhance the general effect.

Double damask table-cloths with matching ample napkins are, for some, the ideal, but need careful laundering,
and an expanse of gleaming white may not work in your
dining room. If it does, wonderful; if it does not, and you
are the fortunate owner of such a cloth, then dye it — but in
a soft shade, as a foil to what is being arranged on it.

Making your own choice when a confusion of ideas is
on offer is difficult. In this book Andrea Spencer helps you
make the right choice for
each occasion with a host
of refreshing and imagin-
ative ideas.

5

FIRST THINGS FIRST

Choosing tableware is one of the most challenging decisions to be made when setting up home. Do you look for quality and a style that won't date, or do you opt for fun and contemporary good looks? There's something to be said for each approach. Maybe you can have the best of both worlds and buy sets of china, glass and table linen to suit different occasions. But don't keep the best of everything locked away in a cabinet. Cherish it, but use it — and enjoy it!

If you want to invest in bone china, silver and crystal, it pays to think hard about the type of design you select. It is wise to go for classic designs which will not lose their appeal or, more important, be discontinued, leaving a gap in your dinner service when the inevitable breakages occur. If, on the other hand, you choose less expensive pottery, you can afford to have fun with fashion.

With cutlery, the choice is between stainless steel, which is available in satin or polished finish, and silver plate, which usually bears the initials EPNS (electroplated nickel silver). Look for cutlery made to British Standard 5577 which guarantees the strength and thickness of any silver plate. Handles may be integral or made from bone, wood, plastic or china but these need extra care if they are not to come adrift. As for glass, whether you collect hand-made full lead crystal or feel safer with tumblers and Paris goblets (the wine glasses most commonly used in restaurants), look for fine rims which are always more pleasant to drink from.

What kind of table linen you buy is also related to the amount you spend. If you are paying over £80.00 for a table-cloth, it makes sense to go for quality (such as linen damask) or craftsmanship (such as a hand-embroidered piece). If you are spending a quarter of that amount, you can safely choose bright colours and bold designs.

Table linen comes in five basic sizes which manufacturers interpret loosely. Table-cloths measure approximately 137 cm (54 in) square, for four people; 137 by 183 cm (54 in by 70 in), for four to six; 137 by 229 cm (54 in by 90 in), for six to eight; 183 cm (70 in) in diameter for round tables seating six people, and 183 by 229 cm (70 in by 90 in) in an oval shape for six to eight diners. The traditional formal table-cloth is made from white linen or cotton damask. (Damask is not a fibre but a reversible, figured fabric.) Lace table-cloths can be used for any style of entertaining. Cotton lace looks crisp but may shrink and needs ironing, while polyester is drip-dry. Polyester-cotton and acrylic fabrics are used for their easy-care qualities. PVC is also used for table-cloths and is invaluable for children's mealtimes.

It is fun to collect old china, glass, silver or lace. It will not often be possible to find pieces that match, but by keeping to a colour theme you can create an original, and ever-changing, series of table settings.

Caring for tableware

Hand-painted china, or ranges decorated with gold, silver or cobalt are often unsuitable for anything but hand-washing as dishwashers may remove the decoration though sometimes a cool programme (under 60°C/140°F) may be used. Cutlery with bone or wood handles also has to be handwashed, and it is not a good idea to put fine crystal into a dishwasher. Apart from the possibility that the glasses will chink together and chip, glass that is constantly cleaned in a dishwasher eventually becomes milky in appearance.

Washing up by hand requires care too. Wash up in a plastic bowl or put a rubber mat in the sink, using hand hot water and a mild detergent. Rinse articles in hot water and dry them in a plastic coated rack before polishing with a soft cloth. The logical order for washing up is glass, cutlery, lightly soiled china, heavily soiled china and saucepans. Change the water when necessary; it is impossible to clean anything in dirty water! To care for fine china, remove leftovers with kitchen paper rather than with a knife, which may scratch, and keep it separate from cutlery when washing-up. A sponge or soft cloth is the best implement to use when washing up, though a soft brush is useful for fluted china and cut glass. Avoid scourers; borax on a soft cloth will remove most tea and coffee stains and a plate powder will shift metal marks.

• Wine glasses should be rinsed in clear water before they are washed. Stains can be removed with a solution of 2 teaspoonsful of ammonia to each glass filled with water.

• Stainless steel and silver plated cutlery should be kept well apart when washing up because silver cleaning solutions will tarnish the 'stainless' steel. Use a proprietary cleaner to remove these marks. The tarnish on silver plate is unsightly but superficial. Remove it with a cleaner containing an inhibitor to keep it at bay for a time.

• All cutlery should be dried as soon as possible after washing up.

• Stains on table-cloths are easily removed provided they are not allowed to set. Blot them up immediately, scrape off any solids and dab gently with plain cool water (add a little detergent for greasy stains). Soak in cold water to loosen the stain, then wash as recommended.

Folding
NAPKINS

Here are three ways of folding napkins to add interest to your table. Like origami, it takes practice to get it right, but the effective results are worth the effort.

The Waterlily

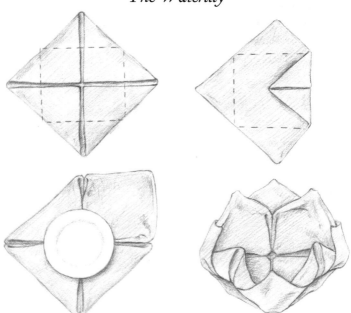

Use a very starched napkin measuring at least 45 cm (18 in) square for the best results. This shape is often used to hold a bread roll.
1.   Fold the napkin in half twice to find the centre. Open out. Fold the corners into the centre. Fold the new corners into the centre.
2.   Turn the napkin over. Bring corners to centre again, and again for the 4th and last time.
3.   Place a small but heavy dish in the middle to hold it down until the lily is complete.
4.   Reach under the folded corners and pull the free sections forward. Pull forward the intermediate leaves and coax them towards the centre.

The Fan

1. Fold a 30 cm (12 in) napkin in half towards you. Make concertina pleats 22 mm (⅞ in) wide to the halfway point with the last fold under the napkin. (This drawing if half size compared with others.)
2. Fold in half again, away from you.
3. Make a diagonal fold towards you leaving a 4 cm (1½ in) flap at the bottom for the support. Fold the flap under the triangle.
4. Open up the fan.

The Bishop's Mitre

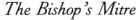

1. Fold napkin in half away from you. Fold the top left hand corner down to the centre, the bottom right hand corner up.
2. Turn the napkin over. With a long side in front of you, fold in half upwards and release the tip under the left-hand fold. Take the extreme right-hand point and tuck it under the left-hand flap.
3. Turn over and slip the left-hand point under the diagonal fold on the right. Stand the napkin up, opening it up from within.

Social niceties are traditionally the responsibility of the hostess rather than the host. The easiest way for her to indicate where she wants her guests to sit is to use place-cards, with a table plan posted in the reception area so that everyone can see where they are sitting and next to whom. This is, however, only appropriate for grand occasions. If, at less formal gatherings, the hostess has a preference about where her guests should sit, she should direct them to their seats — not blithely tell them to sit anywhere and start to intervene when they do as she's said!

At dinner parties, the host sits at the head, the hostess at the end of the table (or opposite each other if it is round). The most important female guest sits next to the host on his right, the most important male guest next to the hostess. (Sometimes it is more tactful to substitute seniority — in terms of age — for importance.) Ideally females should sit next to males, but not if they are married to each other.

This is a rule that is often impossible to implement especially if the numbers of each sex are different. You might prefer to seat your guests next to those you think they will get on with, regardless of gender.

The formal place setting

Cutlery and class consciousness go together, as John Betjeman made clear in 'Phone for the fish knives, Norman', a poetic catalogue of what is Not Done. Many people have little patience with finicky rules but there is some sense in the formal place setting where the cutlery (including the dessert spoon and fork) is placed so that you work from the outside in. The exception is the butter knife which is placed on the inside right.

The soup spoon is often a tablespoon rather than the conventional round bowl design. Any extra cutlery required, such as a sorbet spoon or a snail pick, is brought in with the dish in question. Soup is served in soup plates, not small bowls (which are reserved for lunch when manners are more relaxed) and there is a side plate for toast. The napkin, which should be large, and like the table-cloth, made of white damask, is folded in a triangle or in three like a business letter and placed centrally. Glasses are lined up in order of use working from the inside outwards. Although, to be correct, you should include a sherry glass to accompany the soup, this is not often done today. Next comes the small wine glass for white wine, a large wine glass for red and a flute for champagne to be drunk with the pudding (but which may also be drunk throughout the meal). A plain water goblet may be added.

Salt (nowadays usually rock salt) is served in a small glass dish with a tiny spoon or a silver salt cellar. A pepper mill is acceptable, provided it is not too big.

The general rule is that the less specialized equipment that is used (fish knives for example), the better. The fork is the most important implement. Always use a knife and fork (tines down) together, but never use a spoon without a fork — except for soup or sorbet. By so doing you will avoid censure at banquets, but such formality is not necessary in the home. If you choose to serve bread and butter, the side plate goes to the left and the butter knife is sometimes laid across it rather than on the inside of the place setting. A separate knife should be provided with the butter to transfer butter pats to the side plate. Your own butter knife is used to spread each piece of bread or roll as you break it (with your hands — do not cut it). In most homes, the spoon and fork are laid at the top of the setting nose to tail, simply to save space though strictly speaking this is incorrect. Serving spoons are also laid nose to tail in the centre of the table unless you are serving from the sideboard.

Strict adherence to the rules is used to impress — or intimidate. Rather than make life uncomfortable, make light of the social niceties and concentrate on creating imaginative table settings.

Here, for your edification, is the formal place setting. The dessert spoon (nearest the plate) can be replaced by a fruit knife.

Serving the meal

Careful menu-planning is vital if you are giving a dinner party single-handed. Having a cold starter or pudding and a main course which can be kept waiting if the guests are late will make the whole occasion more relaxed. Remember that soufflés, baked Alaskas and other dishes which need last-minute attention confine you to the kitchen and demand punctuality from your visitors. Even if your guests are assembled in the living room they may take a few crucial minutes to finish their drinks or nip off to the bathroom before taking their places at table.

Ideally, food should be served as soon as it is ready. It is sometimes possible to achieve this by timing the cooking to allow an extra ten to twenty minutes for late arrivals. Punctual guests will not notice the delay provided they are plied with drinks and conversation. Etiquette decrees that guests should arrive a few minutes late and that the meal should begin half an hour after the time for which they were invited so visitors will not expect to eat straightaway.

Keeping food hot

If you want to join your guests for drinks rather than staying in the kitchen, you might consider the following ways of keeping food warm.

A microwave oven will cook vegetables from raw in a few minutes or reheat food in seconds, in the china dishes in which it is to be served, unless these have a gold or silver rim. (Metal must not be used in a microwave.) Although most microwave ovens will take only one dish at a time, you can reheat a second dish in the time it takes to carry the first to the table.

Hot trays and cabinets come into their own at formal dinner parties where food is traditionally served from the sideboard. Although strict convention requires that the dishes are removed immediately, so that there is no question of second helpings, at most dinner parties both the hosts and the guests are more anxious about enjoying the food than satisfying the rules of etiquette. So a hot tray on the sideboard solves the problem of cold second (or third) helpings. Hot cabinets, where the food is warmed inside, can be as expensive as microwave ovens but are not nearly as versatile. Before you buy, consider if the cabinet will suit your style of furniture and whether you will be able to use your own china with it: some of the fitted dishes look like catering equipment. Metal dish warmers which use a nightlight candle are suitable for informal supper parties. Wicker baskets to insulate serving dishes are attractive, but will not keep food warm for long.

Don't forget to warm the plates! If you have a dish-washer, it may have a 'plate warm' programme which uses hot air to heat them. Otherwise use the warming drawer in the oven if there is one, or pre-heat the second oven or grill to the lowest setting, turn off, and put the plates there shortly before serving. Another alternative is to place the plates in a bowl of hot water for five minutes.

How — and whom — to serve

Food is served to the left of each guest and plates are removed from the right. The most important female guest, who sits to the right of the host, is served first. The order of precedence is that unrelated female guests are served first, then relations in order of age — oldest first, females before males. Adults should be served before children, but in practice it is often easier to serve children first, especially if their parents then have to cut up the food for them. At a formal dinner where staff are employed, the most important female is still the first to be served but the waiter or waitress then moves round the table serving each guest in turn, regardless of age, sex or importance. The host (or hostess) is always served last.

Light or dry wines — and this usually means white to accompany *hors-d'œuvres* or fish — are served before red which is poured when the meat course is brought in. The continental habit of eating cheese before pudding allows you to make the most of the red. A sweet white wine is served with pudding, and if you serve cheese after rather than before, this is the time to bring on the port, which should be passed clockwise (to your left), the brandy and liqueurs. Decanting is only necessary for wines with a sediment. White wines should be served chilled (not freezing cold), while red wines are usually opened an hour or two before the meal and at room temperature.

At formal dinners no one is permitted to smoke before the royal toast. This is one rule that can be comfortably translated to mean that no one should smoke between courses. When the coffee is poured guests often retire to the living room and this is the best time to ask the hostess if she has any objection before lighting up. One convention that has almost entirely disappeared dictates that the ladies leave the room while the gentlemen enjoy their brandy and cigars. Ladies are also free to enjoy brandy, and cigars too, if they wish.

PLAIN AND FANCY

This white china has a raised pattern of grapes and vine leaves and a fluted edge. It looks perfect with soft pink but will blend with other pastel coloured tableware too, if the theme is reflected in the flower arrangements. Here we have used roses, but you could use a bowl of hydrangeas to blend with a blue scheme or plants or vines with single flowers scattered amongst them for an eau de nil setting.

Flowers are also used on the napkins, which are simply folded in three and tied with wide satin ribbon, and on the plates, where a small silk flower head is placed at the edge of the second plate and in the centre of the dish. Once again choose colours to suit, with pansies or purple anemones with blue or lily of the valley for green. Bind a spray of flowers for each guest or use a single rose or a tiny pot of wild hyacinths. Cut glass and silver or stainless steel cutlery in a classic design look best with this type of china and you could add to its effect by using a lace cloth over the plain pastel one.

ANYTHING GOES

White china is ideal for supplementing a table set with a variety of pieces of old china. It's rare to find an entire set in any one design, and some of the best bargains consist of a couple of tea cups or an odd number of dinner plates, so white china is invaluable for stretching your collection. When acquiring old china, it's best to choose a theme. Choose either a certain colour, such as the blue shown here, or a motif — roses for example. Or you might collect china in different colours but with the same gold rim which looks particularly effective used with white china to add continuity. Make sure that the accessories are in keeping with the style of the china, using the correct cutlery to accompany Victorian or Art Deco designs.

As the china here is predominantly blue, we set the table with a blue damask cloth and napkins and arranged a posy of blue hydrangeas with a few russet coloured blooms to relate to the secondary colour on the plates. We used silk flowers which won't wilt and die — or go out of season — but you could also dry real hydrangea heads.

BLACK ART

This stylish setting was achieved with basic white china dressed up with strong colours. A fashionable grey table-cloth forms the background decorated with bright yellow flowers to add vibrancy. You could use fresh cut daffodils or chrysanthemums depending on the season, a pot of yellow primulas or silk flowers, as here. The cutlery and the cruets match the cloth, while yellow straws pick out the colour of the flowers.

The china itself is decorated with narrow black ribbon positioned at an angle across the plates. To hold it in place, secure with sticky tape or simply wedge it beneath the rim. Napkins have been folded in the buffet pocket shape (see page 10) and dressed up with a tiny bow. Although we've used black with grey and yellow, it would look just as effective on a plain white cloth and matching napkins — just right for a party on a black and white theme. In this case you would use white flowers with a minimum of greenery, but splashes of red would also be strong enough to offset the black and white.

HERE TODAY...

Transform basic white china with specialist china paint and decorate glasses to match (see page 20). For this setting, we used pretty pastels spattered on to the plates and chose cutlery in soft lemon, pink and blue for an unusual and attractive setting. Glasses with bands of colour and a multi-coloured table emphasize the effect.

The paint was simply flicked on with a toothbrush for a fashionable freehand look. The effect is permanent, but you could use emulsion paint, which would come off in the wash, giving you scope to change the image. Dishes treated this way could only be used for fruit or bread, for example, which would not affect the paint.

To complete the setting, we added a bunch of sweet peas in colours slightly darker than those of the china; they smell as delightful as they look! Tiny multi-coloured sweets pick up the colours of the table-cloth and a single knot of blue ribbon is placed on each plate. You could substitute sugared almonds of assorted shades wrapped in net and tied with ribbon for the sweets shown here.

Painting
CHINA AND GLASS

Stippling and Flicking

Two contrasting colours look cheerful on white china. Screen off the central part of the plate with strips of masking tape laid slightly overlapping, the edges cut clean with a blade. Dip the toothbrush in paint and flick your wrist so that the paint spatters finely over the plate. Leave to dry 24 hours before applying the second colour.

Give glasses a stippled border by flicking paint on from the bristles of a toothbrush with your thumb. Make sure that the glass is perfectly clean before you start. After washing and drying, wipe it over with methylated spirit. Cover the work surface with newspaper. Mix 2 parts cold enamel paint with 1 of hardener in a saucer and leave for 20 minutes to thicken. If it is too thin it will drip. Try out the technique on scrap paper first, to find out how much paint to use and how hard to flick the bristles. Use two tones of one colour for a subtle finish.

Masking

Use transparent colours mixed with thinner for these techniques. By masking off areas and applying paint from an atomizer or airspray gun you can make straight lines with a perfect edge. Stripes, evenly spaced on a flat surface, look dramatic. An interesting variation on glassware is to draw coloured spirals. Use 2 parallel strips of tape for the line, set 2 mm (¹/16 in) apart. Cover the remaining surfaces with newspaper and work from bottom upwards. Leave for 4 hours and apply heat-resisting varnish if the glass will be used for alcoholic drinks.

When working with sprays make sure there is adequate ventilation.

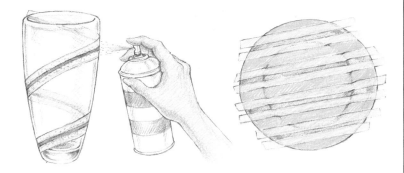

Freehand Painting

Transform a plain white service by embellishing it with your own design. Find a pattern that will work well on both a small plate and a large platter. Using a fine brush, enamel paints and a steady hand, copy the pattern on to each piece, letting each colour dry before starting on the next. Dots can be applied with cotton buds.

WEDDED BLISS

*Simply sensational — a bridal table dressed in white
and covered with net to imitate a wedding veil.
Flowers echo the bride's head-dress, and the simple
cake is surrounded by sprays of fresh and silk flowers
to recall her bouquet. Flowers make a beautiful
setting for the bride and her attendants.*

This is every woman's Big Day, whether the ceremony takes place in church or in a registry office, and the setting for the reception should reflect its importance. The bridegroom traditionally takes second place to the bride, so we make no apology for creating a table based on the bride's gown, veil and flowers. The colours should be chosen to link with the dresses of the bridal party so that those at the reception complement the decorations in the church. If the gown is to be white, nothing is more beautiful than an all-white flower theme as here. Apricot and cream are particularly flattering with an ivory gown and pink looks lovely with magnolia. Follow the theme through by choosing a soft pastel cloth to match but don't attempt to make the bride's bouquet if you are an amateur, for it takes a long training to master the art of wiring flowers.

Often a lot of money is spent on aspects of the wedding which could be better used elsewhere. Take the cake, for example; it's not essential to have an Eiffel Tower of a cake which costs hundreds of pounds. Nothing is better than originality and here is a cake which takes very little time but which looks sensational. We used a simple Genoese sponge, but a fruit cake would be equally suitable. It is a plain, square cake, iced, placed on a silver stand and raised on columns to give it height. The area below is filled with fresh gypsophila and silk flowers, the top is trimmed with silk blossoms and in the centre there's a tiny silver stand holding more fresh gypsophila. A wide ribbon tied in a huge bow makes an appropriate finishing touch.

To create a bridal table setting, we used a plain white sheet decorated with spotted net similar to a wedding veil. It is festooned, or tied in the centre, with a huge satin bow from which hangs a bouquet of white flowers. Champagne is served on a grand mirrored tray decorated with fresh flower heads and ivy; if you can't acquire a tray like this, an oval mirror would work just as well. For a delicate touch, use pink champagne with tiny rose heads floating in the first drinks — perfect for a rose-coloured theme — but make sure the flowers are free from greenfly and remove the flowerheads from the glasses before sipping the champagne!

We used white china with a silver rim which is right for so many formal occasions but plain white catering standard china can look as effective as silver platters if the table is decorated beautifully. Put sandwiches on lace doilies to add a sense of occasion and sprinkle the table with confetti. Don't just fold napkins; roll them in a cornet shape and tie with a narrow strip of white satin ribbon to emphasize the white and silver theme.

Alternatively choose an apricot undercloth with cream organdie and napkins tied with peach coloured ribbons, or pink, another flattering shade. You could also pick out the colour of the pageboys' costumes with blue ribbons interspersed with sprays of roses.

The conventional seating plan at weddings is as follows:

Chief Bridesmaid	Groom's Father	Bride's Mother	Groom	Bride	Bride's Father	Groom's Mother	Best Man

Step-parents are seated at the extreme edge of the table, stepmother next to best man, stepfather next to chief bridesmaid.

This simple cake derives its charm not from scrolls of fussy icing but a single enormous white satin bow to symbolise tying the knot of matrimony, against a profusion of tiny white blooms

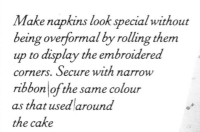

Make napkins look special without being overformal by rolling them up to display the embroidered corners. Secure with narrow ribbon\of the same colour as that used\around the cake

Arranging
FLOWERS

Hidden Supports

The secret of many professional-looking flower arrangements is in the method of support used to keep the individual stems firmly in place. Such supports are essential, particularly with arrangements placed on the dining table to create an eyecatching first impression, but which have to be moved to a side table when the meal is being served and eaten. Whatever method you use to keep the plant material in place, make sure it is completely concealed.

Right *Florist's foams are available in different densities. Dense foam is best for heavy flowers with thick stems, while lighter weights are for delicate specimens.*

Below right *Pin holders are indispensable items of flower arranging equipment, plus special scissors to cut stems cleanly and reel wire for strengthening floppy foliage.*

Below *Crumpled wire netting is an excellent form of support.*

Colour schemes

Summer is the time to make the best of sweet peas in all their fragile colours. They deserve a special container repeating in abstract swirls and stipples their tender shades of lavender, pink and white. No matter if the shape is modern, as long as the china is as delicate as the blooms. Distribute the different colours evenly through the arrangement, which would be ideal for a lunch or afternoon tea.

Mass tulips of one colour together in a goldfish-bowl container for stunning effect, letting the flowers look as if they have arranged themselves artlessly into a shapely group on their arching stems. Use a sparkling clean glass bowl, and top up with fresh water frequently.

For an important dinner party or family gathering such as a wedding, a large and impressive arrangement is a must. Choose a stately container which holds the arrangement high and conceals the supports within. A variety of colours, shapes and sizes is given by cabbage roses, lily of the valley, and stocks, which are arranged with a careful eye to overall proportion and pattern.

A CHILD IS BORN

Although a christening is a more intimate occasion than a wedding, many baptisms now take place during morning service — after which everyone is more than ready to go back to the house for refreshments. Friends are often happy to help with the arrangements, from taking flowers to the church to dressing the table, at this tiring time in the parents' lives; it makes the ceremony more memorable and makes everyone feel involved. Blue for a boy makes a delicate trim to a table setting. Change it to pink or peach for a girl, or use gold, silver, white or aqua, as here, to welcome any baby to the world.

Like weddings, christenings consist of a church ceremony followed by a reception or party, but as it's a less public occasion you can afford to opt for an informal and more colourful style. In church, decorate the font with simple flowers emblematic of childhood and use flowers in season, muting strong colours by using white ribbon. The theme is normally blue for a boy, pink for a girl, but a softer alternative is to substitute peppermint, primrose or peach. The aquamarine used here would be equally suitable for a boy or a girl. It is only really strong colours that look out of place. A cake is essential at a christening but again there's no need to go to great expense. We took a plain iced cake and twisted some filmy aqua-coloured fabric into a knot at the front (chiffon is ideal) and topped it with a stork made from icing whose blue bow was replaced by one in aqua to match. We added scented sweets (cachous) stuck on with a blob of icing sugar in a random pattern round the stork and stood the cake on silver cake columns to give it prominence. Beneath these is a mirror tile which reflects the sachets filled with sugared almonds which guests take home as souvenirs.

To dress the table, use a plain cloth or sheet beneath a lace overcloth or even a lace curtain. Alternatively you can buy lace by the metre, and team it with a coloured undercloth if you prefer. Make bows out of ribbon in the colour of your choice and trim the edge of the table with these, leaving the ends to fall free. Double-sided narrow satin ribbon gives the best effect. Use generous lengths and trim the ends of the ribbons to an inverted V to stop them fraying and to give a neat finish. Choose a spray of simple flowers in the same colour to place in the centre of the table.

When the guests arrive, position the christening presents at the front and, if you like, place the christening cards at the back. Delicate blue and white china is ideal for a christening tea and sweet treats never come amiss, so fill meringues with whipped cream (not the aerosol variety, as it collapses after a few minutes) and decorate with parma violets. For a backdrop, fix a curtain of fine white lawn or dupion and tie back with aqua ribbon. Even the tiniest things are noticed . . . as the star of the show will know.

The first thing you discover when planning a family gathering is that you have too small a table and too few chairs! Only large homes can cater for more than 12 at a sit-down meal though the average house will accommodate 30 or 40 at a buffet party. Here are some ideas to help you cope if you have ten to 15 guests.

Supplement your usual dining table with a garden or occasional table of equal height (the width is not so crucial) to create an L shape. Cover both with matching plain sheets or identical tablecloths. If you have a round or oval dining table, add an extra round garden table to complement it. This is a particularly useful way of seating children.

To make the sachets of sugared almonds, cut out 20 cm (8 in) squares of coloured net, 17.5 cm (7 in) squares of chiffon, 15 cm (6 in) squares of tissue paper and 30 cm (12 in) lengths of narrow ribbon. Lay out the squares with the chiffon sandwiched between the net and the paper. Put 5 or 6 sweets in each pouch. Bring the 4 corners upward simultaneously, grip the neck of the pouch and give it a little twist to hold it while you tie the ribbon in place (another pair of hands is useful for this).

SILVER WEDDING

There's no argument about the most appropriate colour for this table setting! We sprayed fresh fruit and nuts with silver paint and piled them up high in front of candles sprayed with *non-flammable* silver paint in candelabra. A sheer silver table-cloth was used beneath dark grey net; we dabbed patches of glue on this and coated it with glitter before ruching the skirts and holding them in place with silver baubles. If you're short of time, use silver and white or dye a sheet pale grey and team with silver ribbon.

Single flower heads are tied to the napkins with silver ribbon and the white china has a grey and silver rim. The cutlery and condiments are of course . . . silver. Silver

dragees are used for decoration but you could equally well use silver Christmas bells or baubles.

For a buffet, use lots of beautiful foliage such as rosemary, hosta and silver-leaved plants such as senecio and santolina to highlight white and off-white flowers. Place glass or silver candlesticks at intervals down the back of the table with tall white or silver candles and surround the bases with leaves sprayed silver, shaped as a wreath or entwined with ivy, and decorated with tiny silver balls.

For a floral centrepiece, use a block of florists' foam and cover the container with foil. Mount candles on cocktail sticks among the flowers, fixing them above the waterline so the wick does not absorb the moisture. Decorate plain net stencil-fashion by cutting star shapes from cardboard. Lay it over the fabric and spray on aerosol adhesive (available from art shops) then cover with silver glitter.

TROPIC FOR TONIGHT

There's nothing like a house party!
If you're going to the trouble of throwing a party, why
not make it a really memorable occasion by picking a
theme? Guests can join in by choosing clothes to
match; everyone loves to dress up and this is as good
an excuse as any.
Here we show a tropical table setting — hot colours
and cool drinks! Put on a Hawaiian shirt and
Bermuda shorts, pick your desert island discs, pour
yourself a sundowner — and if it's cold outside turn
the heating up, and the lights down . . .

Atmosphere is important to the success of any gathering whether it's for four or 40 guests and it's up to you to set the mood and the style.

Plan well ahead and send out invitations a good three weeks in advance so that guests have plenty of time to organize what they're going to wear to fit in with your theme. Put RSVP at the bottom and include your telephone number to make it easier for those you've invited to reply. Check your guest list a few days beforehand to see exactly how many people you are catering for. Get in supplies at least two days before the party so that if you overlook anything vital you'll find out before the shops are closed. . . . Allow at least one bottle of wine for two people — more if you think they'll need it — and don't assume your guests will have dined before they arrive. Lay on plenty of cheap, filling foods to absorb the alcohol so that no one becomes unintentionally drunk.

Decorate the room and dress the table the day before. There is nothing worse than a last minute flap. If you are pushed for time, dress yourself and the table first; no one will notice if the food is delayed.

Decide what type of music you will need (it should be in keeping with the theme of the party) and make up a good selection of tapes so that it plays without a break; good music gets a party going. In this instance you could choose reggae or a steel band . . . or *Blue Hawaii*. See that the house is warm and inviting when guests start to arrive but that there is adequate ventilation when the party gets into full swing; a lot of people generate a lot of heat.

If it's going to be a large party in a public room, you'll have to decide how to deal with gatecrashers. Ask your friends to bring their invitations and hire someone to check them (and to look after the coats) as a deterrent.

Dressing the table

Hot colours such as bright pinks, sky blues, sunshine yellows and lush greens form the basis of this scheme. Lay tablecloths, lengths of fabric or crepe paper in the colours you choose diagonally so that their points form an attractive edging to the table and make co-ordinating napkins into exotic lilies — instructions on page 10.

Food and drink should be appropriate to the occasion, so prepare heady fruit cocktails (with tropical squash for drivers and non-drinkers) and put them into hollowed-out fresh pineapples taking care not to split the skin; if in doubt put a tumbler inside. Dress up cocktail glasses with brightly coloured parasols or plastic palm trees and decorate the table with exotic fruit kebabs stuck into half a pineapple or grapefruit. (Coat the fruit first in one of the special products designed to prevent discolouration.) Finally, arrange the flower heads and garlands which can also be used to decorate the walls — or perhaps yourself.

Other party themes could be inspired by colours, like black and white, with guests dressed to match and a table laid with black bread, mock caviar and even black-eyed peas. Choose either a table-cloth made from a length of black fabric or a white one decorated with black ribbons. Country music fans will appreciate a home-on-the-range approach, and love dressing the part. Or arrange a rock 'n' roll party with hamburgers, girls in pony tails and pumps and men in slicked hairstyles and brothel creeper shoes!

Cut out squares of brightly coloured tissue paper measuring approximately 15 x 15 cm (6 x 6 in). Fold in quarters and twist the inner corner — the centre of the square — downwards. Thread the squares in alternating colours on to a 1.2 m (48 in) length of cotton and flounce them outwards like petals. Trail the garlands around and along the front of the table or join the ends so that intoxicated guests can fling them round their necks.

COMING OF AGE

Whether coming of age is celebrated at 18 or at the grand old age of 21, it's bound to be an exciting and lively occasion. Times have changed and so has the style of parties; a sedate setting is unlikely to go down well, and the emphasis will be on loud music, flashing lights and even a complete (if temporary) change of decor.

Use strong, abstract shapes and bright, almost iridescent colours and arrange for a display of coloured lights to play over the surfaces. We used black paper with holes punched in it through which the coloured lights shine, but you could use branches painted white or black entwined with fairy lights so that they cast shadows to give depth to the background. Mobiles in geometric shapes suspended from the lights will move on their own in the heat, adding a new dimension to the scene. For extra effect, run fairy lights round the edge of the table but be sure the wires do not trail where guests are likely to trip over them.

This occasion demands a special cake and here is something quite out of the ordinary. We covered a box with mirrorflex (sections of mirror on a felt backing) but a polished tin would work just as well. Inside is the plain cake, waiting to be cut when required, and on top is a toy car sprayed silver. A compact disc is fixed to this, angled to catch the light, and the front of the ensemble is decorated with shocking pink foil which has stars stamped out — for the star of the party. The corners of the cake are decorated with silver baubles for definition and to give it height it stands on four silver cake pillars.

The table top is black plastic on which flakes of iridescent material have been scattered. (This is available from display shops and is on sale more widely at Christmastime.) It catches the light, and the effect is reflected by the black plastic. Black paper plates are used for co-ordination and drama, with sophisticated cocktails for glamour and plain glasses for those who prefer wine. You can also change the lighting considerably by using coloured bulbs or gels (sheets of coloured acetate used in stage lighting) clipped to the top of lamps.

BIRTHDAY TREATS

*Children get as much fun
from helping to arrange their parties as they do from
the birthday itself. Look for inspiration from the
child's favourite book or television programme and
incorporate the figures in the table setting. Many
popular characters are available on paper plates and
cups but plain tableware is just as effective if you
choose the bright colours and simple shapes which
characterize children's books. Here the Disney theme
is repeated in the tiny toys and bright colours.*

We can all remember when birthdays were eagerly anticipated and a six-week countdown to the big day was the norm! Make use of the waiting time and the mounting excitement to work out a theme and 'cook up' something special. Children love bright colours so the brighter the table the better they'll like it. It's bound to be a bit of a disaster area by the time they've finished so cover the table with crepe paper or, as we've done here, use a bright table-cloth topped by a couple of metres (yards) of clear plastic and put a pile of wax crayons in the middle to keep little hands busy while waiting for or finishing their food. The plastic will also protect the table from the inevitable spills. To save breakages — and washing up — use paper plates and beakers with striped bendy straws.

Presents always play a big part, so make up little parcels like tiny Dick Whittington bags. Here the Walt Disney theme was carried through with small characters and badges for the children to take home and best of all, masks to wear at the table.

Small children will rarely eat more than crisps, cold sausages and ice cream, but older ones like something more substantial — fish fingers and chips, or hamburgers for an all-American menu! They'd be disappointed though if there were no mounds of sandwiches and cakes, and the birthday cake is always the centre of attention. Rather than going to the expense of buying a novelty cake or spending hours making our own, we bought a simple round one, clad it in glacé icing and tied a huge red bow round the middle. As a finishing touch tiny windmills were inserted at the edge of the ribbon to spin round when the candles are blown out. Take care when buying non-extinguishable candles. They look wonderful and burn like tiny sparklers but be sure to have a bowl of water nearby and a pair of tweezers so that you can remove them quickly — they burn down very fast and you can't put them out by snuffing or even standing on them. Children love sweets so make some centrepieces like the nest of chocolate thins filled with sugared almonds or tiny eggs or a jar of star-shaped lollipops.

Place cards are a good idea as they avoid arguments over who sits where. Get your child to help you; all you need is a piece of card about 5 cm (2 in) long folded in half so that it stands up. Decorate them with cartoon characters in keeping with your chosen theme which can be cut out of comics or trace a picture for your child to colour in.

As a background we've used spotted fabric beneath clear plastic with polka dot material for the loot bags and even spotted ribbon to tie them with. Carrying an idea through like this makes all the difference to the table setting. You could choose a time theme, for example, with a clock cake whose hands point to the number marking the child's age and give toy watches as presents. Another easy idea is a train cake made from chocolate Swiss rolls and a train set running round the table. And make sure there are lots of balloons!

While the table bearing goodies should look crammed, colourful and inviting, the setting for a children's party should be spacious and safe. A large non-slippery floor area with cushions is best, for playing musical chairs, pass the parcel or blind man's buff. And these days, music is a must. Cassettes of nursery songs sung with gusto keep the partymakers merry until mums come to take them home.

Make a simple round, iced white cake sensational with an enormous silky bow. Add miniature windmills, coloured candles in choo-choo train holders and a circle of bright jelly beans. In the middle, Mickey waves 'Happy Birthday' to the party girl or boy

For the take-home bags, use remnants of fabric cut up into 20 or 30 cm (8 or 12 in) squares, tied at the top. Attach them to 30 cm (12 in) garden canes with ribbon tied in a floppy bow. Plump the bags out with tissue paper, which will protect the presents inside

BACKSTAGE PLANNING

To seat guests numbering between 15 and 30 you will need to hire trestle tables and folding or stacking chairs or benches. You may be able to borrow them from a local church hall or scout group in return for a donation to funds, but remember that you will have to provide transport. The larger catering equipment firms will hire tables and chairs as well as cutlery, china, glass and linen — see your local Yellow Pages for details.

Another option is to use pasting tables, which can be papered in a wallcovering design to emphasize the theme of the party or the decor (use a water-resistant vinyl if possible), painted, or covered in foil. Pasting tables are cheap but flimsy and won't withstand heavy weights, so organize a separate side table for drinks, plates and cutlery and serve food from a sideboard if you are planning a sit-down meal.

Glasses can often be loaned from the off-licence or wine merchant which supplies the drink. A refundable deposit may be charged.

If you have invited as many as 30 to 100 guests it may be wise to consider hiring a marquee to cope with these numbers at home. The cost varies from around £400 for a marquee for 150 guests to £1200 plus for the same number if you want lighting, a dance floor and equipment. Look under Tent and Marquee Hire in the Yellow Pages for firms in your area.

Alternatively, rent a private room in a pub, club, hotel or village hall; colleges and schools may also offer this facility. Pubs and hotels will stipulate that they supply you with food and drink; in other venues you will have to provide your own or employ a separate catering firm. These vary in the type of equipment they provide as some have a more comprehensive range than others. Specialists like wedding firms will undertake to lay on everything you require, from food and drink to the wedding cake and even the wedding dress.

If you set out to furnish a hall or marquee for the occasion, allow one 6ft table for every 25 guests. Extra glasses are always necessary to cater for the inevitable breakages and forgetful guests who 'lose' their drinks. Additional napkins, whether paper or linen, will be needed for the same reason and to deal with spills. You may also require staff (use a reputable employment agency which specializes in catering work). Allow one helper per 20 guests.

Remember to book rooms or equipment well in advance especially if you are planning your party on a Saturday or at a popular time like Christmas or New Year. Some hotels are booked for wedding receptions a year in advance! Get confirmation of the date, price, and what is included in writing, and for further peace of mind, consider having hired equipment delivered a day early. This will give you extra time to arrange everything, but of course you will incur extra expense.

Novelties

If you want an unusual location for a party, anniversary celebration or wedding celebration, try hiring one of the following:

Train — or at least a first class carriage or two. The cost, without catering, is £2,000 plus, but if you are interested, contact the Divisional Manager at the regional office of British Rail for your area.

Bus — double deckers can often be hired without seats on the lower deck and luxury coaches now have videos, w.c.s and catering facilities. Apply to your local bus company or coach hire firm.

Boat — look up 'Boat proprietors and hire' in Yellow Pages or ask the English Tourist Board to send you their listings for the area you have in mind. You can hire anything from a cabin cruiser or narrow boat to a floating restaurant to cater for 150 guests.

Stately home — write direct to the stately home you are interested in or apply to the National Trust, 36 Queen Anne's Gate, London SW1H 9AS.

Invitations and place cards

Make your own invitations to link with the theme of your party. A drawing or cartoon by you or a friend can be reproduced by any printer. A sketch of your new house would be right for an invitation to a house-warming; a cartoon would set the scene for a birthday or anniversary party. The same sketch could be shown in miniature on place cards.

Alternatively, cut a simple shape from card using a template. Buy postcards with appropriate pictures and use Letraset (available from art shops) to give your message a professional finish.

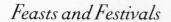

ALL THINGS BRIGHT...

Easter is associated with new life, for the Bible reminds us of the Resurrection while Easter eggs symbolize birth and continuity. It marks the beginning of spring, when the bright colours of daffodils, tulips and forsythia make a welcome contrast to the dullness of winter. Use these flowers to decorate an informal Easter table to celebrate the season. Nests of eggs are the perfect centrepiece. Make one out of dried grass and place marzipan eggs in it. Here is a table set for Easter with spring flowers surrounding china in yellow, white and blue to match.

Easter is synonymous with eggs, which are traditionally dyed in bright colours. As eggshells are absorbent, avoid chemical dyes: instead use food colouring added to the water in which you boil the eggs, or wrap the egg in the outer skin of an onion for a delicate dapped effect. To create a pattern, trace a design on the shell with the point of a candle before it is dyed or squiggle a cartoon on the egg with indelible felt tip to represent the member of the family it's intended for.

We've repeated the rounded shapes of the eggs in the circular table-cloth, an interesting combination of fine fabric and tiny bows. (See page 68 for instructions on making a round table-cloth.) A nice idea for any Easter table is to use three cloths of varying diameters in toning colours on top of each other to give a tiered effect — say pale blue, then lavender and lemon for the top cloth. You don't have to buy new cloths — use old white sheets and dye them using one of the hot or cold water dyes now available in a range of colours.

The napkins are in different colours to blend with the scheme, folded in four, rolled up and tied with ribbon in a simple knot. A bunch of spring flowers in a jug forms a pretty table centre and the crockery is fine and light, incorporating the blue and yellow of the flowers and table linen and offset by cutlery with white handles.

Like Christmas, Easter is both a secular and a religious festival; indeed of the two it has greater importance in the church calendar. Its particular rituals — the lighting of the Easter candle, the christening of a newborn baby, the ending of the dark days of Lent — remind us that this is a time to celebrat new life in a new year. Yellow and blue, innocent and bright as the spring sun in a clear sky, are the perfect colours to set the scene. There is an abundance of flowers to continue this theme. One of the nicest ways of using them, if you can plan far enough ahead, is to plant a bowl with dwarf iris and narcissi — varieties that reach about 15 cm (6 in) high — ready to bloom at Eastertime. Their tiny flowers will be seen to best advantage at close quarters. Other blue flowers breaking forth now include scilla, grape hyacinths and some strains of polyanthus; for yellow look to tulips and shrubs like forsythia and corylopsis.

Don't forget that Easter has its own cake, too (if you have room for it after indulging in hot cross buns). Simnel cake, rich with currants, spices and marzipan, is a delicious reward after the deprivations of Lent.

On the table are small wreaths of flowers encircling the plates and intertwining with each other. These are very realistic silk flowers but you could make something similar from dried flowers. Make a circle from medium gauge wire and fix the flowers on to it with reel wire. Silk flowers with wire stems make this even easier.

Decide on the length of wire you will need for making the circlets by laying a setting and curving the wire around it. Leave enough room to make it look as if the plate is nestling in the flowers. Wind fine wire round the stems of the flowers and attach them to the ring, covering it completely.

HARVEST HOME

Thanksgiving for the harvest is one of the oldest and most joyous of festivals. Hire a hall or borrow a barn if your living space is cramped, and invite the world, his wife and their children too, heaping the boards with the good things that summer has produced in a simple style which makes everyone feel happy and relaxed. Stack a variety of loaves in great tumbling mounds on the table, with a special harvest loaf as a centrepiece if you can persuade a friendly baker to create this traditional work of art. Fill baskets and bowls with apples and pears and decorate the room with huge pitchers of flowers and sheaves of grasses. Be sure to make room for a corn dolly, a fertility symbol traditionally made from the last of the corn, cut ceremonially and with great respect.

In keeping with the rustic mood, arrange trugs or baskets filled with the finest-looking fruits and vegetables — the rosiest apples, greenest cabbages, plumpest marrows and the most succulent tomatoes and leeks — on a linen cloth or a piece of old lace. Team earthenware jugs and heavy glasses with pewter, stoneware and wooden dishes, plus silver cutlery in Old English designs and lace-edged napkins. Use yellow dahlias and russet chrysanthemums, informally arranged to accompany the spread.

To complete this scene of plenty use lots of church candles to cast a mellow glow. Consider making small stooks of corn, reminiscent of those brought in from the fields, tied up with gingham or russet coloured ribbon for table decorations. Alternatively use bunches of autumn leaves, or make garlands either by threading fruit and vegetables on to strings or wiring on leaves and berries. Serve coarse pâté, cheese, fruit and scrumpy cider to remind everyone of the meaning of harvest home.

Halloween

Tradition has it that on the evening of the last day of October witches and ghosts are abroad — an excuse for a wonderfully weird table setting. To make a suitably ghoulish background, black crêpe paper was used. Black plates and silver stars decorate the table and black tape curls round glasses which contain a potent-looking but innocent brew of orange juice tinged with cochineal.

For spooky lanterns, hollow out a turnip or pumpkin. Cut holes for the eyes and a jagged line for the mouth. Place a nightlight low down inside.

To make the witches' hats, cut a quarter-circle shape from the point at the edge of some black card, then wrap the base round to form a cone and stick with tape or staple. Decorate with silver stars.

Apple bobbing is a perennial favourite: place the apples in a bowl of water and tie contestants' hands behind their backs. The aim is to take a bite from an apple without swallowing a mouthful of water.

REMEMBER, REMEMBER

On Guy Fawkes Night after the bonfire and fireworks guests will be ready for hot drinks and baked potatoes. It's a good idea to join forces with friends and neighbours to organize a communal display. Set a splendid table with a cloth made from red crepe paper cut into flame shapes along the edge and orange crepe paper underneath. Make a centrepiece from sparklers and light them when all the guests are assembled (but don't use outdoor sparklers if you're holding the feast indoors). Make a huge bowl of punch to welcome guests and ward off the chill. Choose red handled cutlery, and plastic or paper plates.

Robust food that can easily be eaten with fingers is best. Shiny toffee apples are easy to make: mix four parts sugar to one part water and cook, stirring all the time, until it turns into toffee. Fix the sticks into the apples, pour the toffee over and allow to set hard.

N.B. Take care with fireworks, candles, lighted matches and so on at all times, particularly when close to the crepe paper cloths.

But Once a Year

*A traditional approach to Christmas instantly creates
a festive atmosphere. Roaring log fires, carols, angels
(or even angelic children) and the traditional colours
of red and green set the scene, but it's one that can be
adapted to suit your own special style. Choose a
theme, and a colour scheme, and use them
throughout the house, from evergreens looped round
the fireplace and tied up with satin bows to the
garlands twined round the banisters and the wreaths
which form table decorations and give a warm
welcome at the front door.*

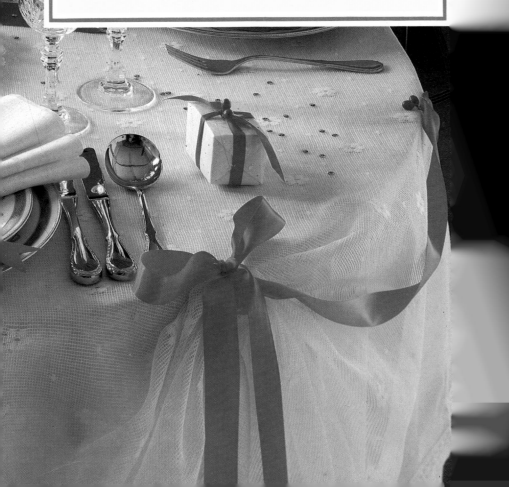

Deck the hall — and the dining room too — with boughs of holly, a traditional protection against fire and storms, plus mistletoe, laurel and even rosemary and bay, which should be brought into the house on Christmas Eve and taken down by Twelfth Night. Remember that flowers and foliage dry out quickly in centrally heated homes, and as the Christmas break is a long one, spray the arrangements regularly and move them into cooler rooms when they are not needed.

To make a wreath for a centrepiece or door which will survive the holiday, wrap a wire frame in moss (for indoor use wrap the moss in cling film to keep the moisture in and place it on a plate or tray so that it won't mark the table) then push strips of evergreen into this and bind them on with florists' wire. If the wreath is intended as a table centre, arrange candles in the middle which add height and make it more of a focal point.

The Christmas tree will also need watering — at least a pint (half a litre) a day — and as this is a busy time of year you might prefer to invest in one of the very realistic plastic or silk trees on the market; artificial flowers, holly and mistletoe are also available. The initial outlay is quite expensive if you choose a convincing tree, so take care when you buy not to limit your scheme as you might want to try a different approach next year.

For the tabletop, nothing looks more inviting than a white cloth decorated with red and green. If you don't have a large cloth then use a white sheet topped by a lace cloth or even a lace bedspread or curtains as here. If you prefer a pink and green scheme to red, place a pink sheet under the lace and use co-ordinating ribbon. Ruche up the lace at each corner: here it is fastened with silky bows but fir cones, small bells and baubles would look equally attractive and crepe paper garlands or paper chains made by the children are in keeping with the season. We twisted the ribbon and attached it to the cloth with two or three large stitches before putting the bows in place. Large damask napkins, about 60 cm (24 in) square, were folded in concertina fashion. The tops were fanned out to make them look more effective and the napkins were tied with ribbon to which a fabric poinsettia was attached, to be taken home as a souvenir of the event. Place cards are simply folded in the middle and decorated with ribbon and a couple of fake berries. By each place there is also a little present, again tied up with red ribbon. A plate of chocolate holly to follow the feast was made by greasing holly leaves and coating with melted cooking chocolate. When the chocolate hardens, peel off the leaf and dust with icing sugar to look like snow.

Lastly, sprinkle the table with tiny green sequins which sparkle in the candlelight. As an alternative to the customary circle of evergreens and candles in the centre of the table, make a splendid pyramid of fruit, which can be eaten with the cheese. For the greatest visual impact, limit yourself to a single variety, perhaps a mound of green grapes, or red apples, polished to perfection.

The table centre, a simple wreath of holly and ivy, is studded with red and white rose and clusters of cotoneaster berries. The three church candles in the middle are firmly set in holders concealed by foliage. You should set the centrepiece on a small tray to protect your best table linen from drips of candle wax.

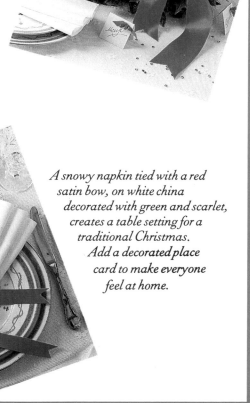

A snowy napkin tied with a red satin bow, on white china decorated with green and scarlet, creates a table setting for a traditional Christmas. Add a decorated place card to make everyone feel at home.

Making
DECORATIONS

Table Swag

Plan the design well in advance to make sure you get enough plant material. You will need enough 6-mm (¹/4-in)-thick cord or rope to go round the table in a series of shallow loops. Pin it into place and mark the fixing points and the centre of each loop with a piece of thread. The base of the swag is formed from evergreens such as ivy and cupressus, bound into sprays about 15 cm (6 in) long with wire. Wire the stems of each bunch to the swag, starting from the outside edge and working towards the centre. The stems should point towards

the centre so that each bunch covers the stems of the one before. Fill in any gaps with spare evergreens. Dot with flower heads or tiny bunches of flowers bound with wire, tucking the stems into the background and fixing with wire. Attach the swag to the table with drawing pins or sew it into place. Conceal the fixing points with large blooms and finish with bows to tone with the flowers and table-cloth.

Centrepieces

Use as your base a flat metal cake tin about 30-37.5 cm (12-15 in) in diameter. Weave together six 45 cm (18 in) lengths of medium gauge stub wire (available from florists') to make a circle and fix it to the base with dabs of plasticine. Attach holly leaves with reel wire to cover the ring. With plasticine, fix one block of dampened foam for each candle in the centre. Put the candles in place and insert flower heads, berries and foliage wound with reel wire into the foam. The base must be completely hidden and the wreath look good from every angle. Make a separate bow and attach it with fine thread or wire. If you use silk flowers and artificial leaves and berries the wreath may be used again; only the candles will need replacing.

Above *Make a candle wreath for a wedding or special birthday using wire and shaped blocks of foam.*

A Christmas Cracker

Are you bold enough to break with the conventional Christmas? Here are some exciting alternatives.

This table is dressed with electric blue and black, but you could combine pink and white, yellow and black or silver and grey to suit your scheme. In place of the standard Christmas tree we requisitioned a bay tree and decorated it with fairy lights. You could use a Kentia palm instead, or a branch sprayed black or silver which could be dressed with baubles.

Let loose with the spray can, we sprayed everything silver, candles too, using a non-inflammable aerosol suitable for spraying cars. We sprayed nuts silver and placed them to the side of the table, each cushioned in a net frill which also trims the crackers. For the centrepieces we used baubles by themselves on a cake stand in silver and blue, interspersed with silvered nuts. Blue ribbon was run the length of the table in two strips to define the section containing the nuts and the centrepiece, but choose the colour which fits your theme. Bright blue napkins were folded into simple rectangles and silver stars were

sprinkled over the table, which could be covered in black shawls or scrunched-up net.

To make the party go with a bang, we dressed up plain crackers with frilled collars of silver-trimmed blue net (see instructions below). Tie the collars on to the necks of each cracker with fine thread or shirring elastic before decorating them with blue or silver trimmings of your choice.

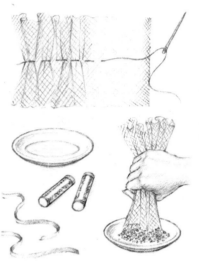

For the cracker collars, cut rectangles of net 15 x 25 cm (6 x 10 in) and sew a row of gathering stitches down the centre. Draw up the thread and secure to make a frill. Dip the ends in a saucer of clear-drying glue, then in glitter. Tap off the excess. Attach to the crackers and finish with knots of narrow blue ribbon.

IN WITH THE NEW

Overflowing into the New Year is Hogmanay, the last day of the dying year. Continue the Scottish theme with the First Footing, when a tall dark male visitor brings bread, coal and salt into the house after midnight to ensure prosperity in the year ahead. The whole evening revolves around the clock. Everyone waits for the hands to point to midnight, the signal for glasses to be raised to welcome the New Year. Prospect for gold with pink for fun, now and in the future.

Informal Entertaining

ANYONE FOR SUMMER?

Green and gardens go together, and a combination of white and green on a table set for a summer lunch looks fresh and cool when the heat is on . . . There is a vast selection of fresh flowers to choose from at this time of year to deck out a garden table, offset by trees and shrubs outdoors or by houseplants and bunches of foliage indoors to transform any dining room into a leafy conservatory. Capture summer in a table setting of green and white where the angles of the mirror and slatted garden table are offset by the curves of plates and petals.

The theme is continued by the china with its fine green rim and cutlery with dark green porcelain handles. Inside the plates, the white china dishes have interesting shapes which more than make up for the absence of pattern. Even the glasses have a green hue. Try a first course of avocado in a simple dressing to please the eye while tempting the palate! Crisp salads gleaming with a touch of lemon and olive oil and the generous use of fresh herbs are a delight to look at while the glasses are just waiting to be filled with chilled white wine. Add a sprig of mint, borage, or lemon verbena to summer cocktails or freeze the leaves inside ice cubes, and garnish ice-cream with lemon verbena which serves as an edible decoration. As an alternative to avocado, try vichyssoise topped by finely chopped chives which also emphasizes the colour scheme.

The idea of foliage in glass is repeated by the centre-piece made from white hydrangea heads set in a goldfish bowl. They are set on a mirror to reflect the light and to double their impact. Potted shrubs are placed close to the table to bring the garden indoors, an idea to which the white slatted table also contributes. If you want to use a conventional dining table, cover it with a plain white cloth for a similar look. For a more intimate effect outdoors, group several small tables together rather than laying one large one.

You can choose from a wealth of white flowers. Lightly scented white roses would look beautiful and sprays of philadelphus will fill the air with their perfume. Use them for lunch on the terrace rather than a meal served indoors, as their scent may conflict with the food. Daisies would look equally attractive in this informal setting or you could substitute a small group of cacti whose exotic flowers and shapes would be emphasized by the mirror below. Scatter flower heads in small bowls as an alternative centrepiece, and dot them in the dishes for guests to transfer to their hair — or lapels. Blue or violet flowers would make appropriately cool alternatives.

Top of the Morning

If the occasion is simple, the presentation should follow suit. Many families now eat in their kitchens and entertain guests there and it's certainly the most convenient place to have breakfast. It could be served on a scrubbed stripped pine table, or, as here, on a gingham cloth with brown pottery or white china with a touch of colour. As an alternative to blue you could use pink and white check for a pretty effect, red for a jolly atmosphere or yellow for warmth. Choose simple flowers to match, like the white daisies used to adorn this table.

Keep croissants or toast warm by tying them up in a square of fabric to match the cloth. Shown here is a simple square of cotton tied in a knot on top and decorated with daisies. The yellow centres of the daisies are picked up by the glasses of orange juice and the rich brown of the boiled eggs which contrast with the cool blue table linen. We made the cloth, mats and napkins from fabric bought by the metre. They look charming and are very easy to make as the feature on pages 68-9 describes.

Making
TABLE LINEN

Circular Table-Cloth

If you enjoy sewing, you can make table-cloths which cost less than bought ones in fabrics which relate to the other soft furnishings in the room.

The diameter of the cloth should be the same as the table plus 45 cm (18 in) minimum plus a 12 mm (1/2 in) hem.

1. Fold the fabric in quarters, wrong side out. Cut out a piece of paper the same size as the folded fabric. Tie a length of string to a pencil. Measure the string to give you the radius of the cloth. Pin the string to a corner of the paper and with the string taut, draw a quarter circle. Cut round the pencil line. This is your paper pattern.
2. Pin the pattern to the folded fabric as shown, with the right angle at the centre of the folds. Cut along the curved edge through all the thicknesses of fabric. Remove the pattern and open out the material.
3. Snip the raw edge at 6 mm (1/4 in) intervals to make it easy to hem. Turn the hem and baste-stitch into place. For a neat finish, cover the hem with bias binding, attached with a double row of machine stitching.

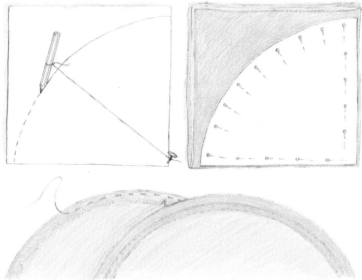

Place Mats

The easiest placemats to make are rectangular, using quilted fabric, measuring about 20 x 30 cm (8 x 12 in). You can also quilt your own fabric using polyester wadding between the two sides. Simply trim with bias binding. Fold the binding in half and press. Tuck the raw edges of the mat inside the fold and tack into place. Slipstitch the cut edges of the binding together. To finish, hand- or machine stitch close to the edge of the binding and remove the tacking.

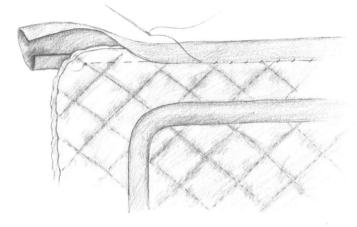

Napkins

Napkins usually measure from 25 cm (10 in) square to more than double that size. There are several ways to finish the edge.

1a)   Zigzag along a double hem first along one side, then turn the napkin over and zigzag over the original row of stitching.

1b)   Finish a double hem with two rows of straight machine stitching.

2a)   Delicate fabrics trimmed with lace look pretty at teatime.

2b)   To make a fringed edge, simply fray the fabric to an even depth all round and secure with a single row of machine stitching.

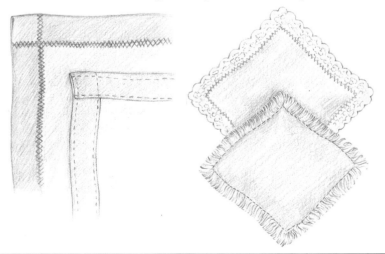

ALL TOGETHER, NOW

This is the day when lunch traditionally replaces dinner as the most important meal. It provides an opportunity for even the tiniest members of the family to socialize and to realize that the occasion is as important as the food! They don't need special equipment apart from a high chair (the tall Windsor chairs which pull up to the table are ideal as they help small children to take part in the proceedings) and small-scale cutlery.

Lunch will usually be late and leisurely. Choose a happy colour for the table setting like this warm yellow which puts everyone in a sunny mood. Instead of placing a large flower arrangement at the centre of the table which might interfere with conversation and get in the way of the dishes, we placed daffodil heads in small glasses and put one into each of the soup bowls. The cutlery has yellow handles to match and the china has a pale yellow rim. It's an informal setting to accompany the traditional menu but the white damask cloth, napkins and silver cruets give a real sense of occasion. This cloth has a self pattern along the border of the table, but you can pretty up a plain one, with coloured ribbons run down the length of the table.

The glasses we used here are chunky goblets (children could be given matching tumblers or bright yellow beakers for their drinks). If you are entertaining a large number, transfer two-litre bottles of supermarket wine into a decanter. It's not only easier to pour but looks more elegant. You may need to add placemats for serving dishes if you are dishing up direct from a casserole. You could choose plain yellow to blend with the scheme or simple rush mats to echo the cane of the dining chairs.

Adapt the setting to suit the formality of the occasion and the age of the participants. If you are entertaining uncles and aunts, bring out your cut-glass and fine china, using the same snowy cloth that's shown here. If your guests are friends with young children, consider putting a sheet of polythene beneath the top cloth to protect your table from major spills, and if you have a young family yourself, you may find it worthwhile to buy a cloth which has a poly-cotton top and a PVC backing, combining elegance with practicality. Choose simple earthenware crockery and give children pudding plates or soup bowls for their food so that they feel really grown up.

Sunday lunch is often the only meal of the week when all the family get together and exchange news of what is happening in their lives. It becomes a pleasant and relaxing ritual that deserves to be celebrated with touches of formality that may be overlooked at every-day meals. A few flowers, for example, can have a transforming effect.

MORNING COFFEE

Compared to the intimacy of family meals, a coffee morning is a public affair but an easy way to extend your circle of acquaintances. Show off a collection of old china while friends exchange news and views. It's still possible to pick up tiny translucent coffee cups and saucers at a reasonable price — don't worry if they are not all the same. Try to link them by colour instead and choose an imposing coffee pot to add distinction. Collect tiny silver coffee spoons or egg spoons to suit the size of the cups or look for the little 'apostle' spoons traditionally given as christening or confirmation presents. Pick out the dominant colours in your china for the table-cloth and flower arrangement but choose soft patterns and fragile blooms.

You can stretch this assortment by using companion cups in a plain colour; blue or pink would suit the china shown here. Look for bone china with a pretty detail like fluting or gilded rims to give coherence to your collection.

FIRESIDE TEA

Tea-time is a truly British ritual. It's a time for drawing the curtains on chilly winter nights, turning on the lights, building up a blazing fire and eating hot buttered scones, crumpets or fruit cake. The children can help lay the table or tray, arrange the flowers and even ice a few biscuits or fill the jam tarts. Choose fine china (nothing tastes better than piping hot tea from delicate china cups) patterned with flowers such as roses or apple blossom. Set the table with a lovely lace cloth and white or pastel napkins and make a small posy of flowers as a centrepiece. Serve jam or honey and cream in glass dishes with pretty spoons and remember to warm the teapot before making the tea!

If you don't possess a lace table-cloth, pretty up the plates with paper doilies underneath the cakes or scones. Alternatively use plain white china and add a flowered table-cloth, either printed or embroidered, but make sure that the colours and patterns are as delicate as the china.

A Moveable Feast

' "There's cold chicken inside it," replied the Rat
briefly; "coldtonguecoldhamcoldbeefpickled-
gherkinssaladfrenchrollscresssandwidgespottedmeat-
gingerbeerlemonadesodawater — "
"O stop, stop," cried the Mole in ecstasies: "This is
too much!"
"Do you really think so?" inquired the Rat seriously.
"It's only what I always take on these little
excursions; and the other animals are always telling
me that I'm a mean beast and cut it very fine!" '

The Wind in the Willows *by Kenneth Grahame*

As Mole found out, there's no need to limit yourself to sandwiches and a flask of coffee when planning a picnic. Increasing numbers of people have discovered the pleasures of an Edwardian style cold collation stowed in a wicker hamper and eaten from china plates — and if soft drinks aren't your style, washed down with a glass of crisp white wine. Don't forget the bottle-opener! Other essentials include plain water and food that's easy to eat. Fresh air really does stimulate the appetite, it seems. Most people can manage a slice of cake by the end of the afternoon.

For a really successful picnic you will also need that modern invention, the cool bag, to keep wine and other beverages cold or to keep dishes warm on a chilly day. You will have to be prepared to make the best of the weather, so take a parasol to protect you from the sunshine so that you can curl up in its shade for a nap after lunch and rugs to sit on, or to wrap yourself in if the weather suddenly turns chilly.

It's worth choosing your picnic spot with care. You don't want to be bothered by too many flies, or cows, or people, but on the other hand you won't want to walk too far with your feast. Look for a sunny spot protected from wind by banks or trees which also provide a natural backdrop. Water in the form of a river or stream is an added bonus, but avoid stagnant ponds or slow-flowing brooks which attract midges.

Take the trouble to make the meal a special occasion by selecting equipment to complement your surroundings. Here the theme is pastels to blend with the parasols, but you could use the vivid red and green found in many tartan travelling rugs. Rugs form the most comfortable ground sheet-cum-tablecloth. Add a couple of cushions and a cloth made from PVC which is easily wiped down.

Pleasant as it is to use china and proper cutlery rather than the flimsy plastic kind, if transport is a problem substitute paper plates in pastel colours to suit your colour theme. This saves carrying dirty dishes home and washing them up afterwards; take a plastic bag or bin liner with you and simply put your used paper plates into the nearest wastebin.

To make organization easier we designed these attractive placemats which are just as useful for a buffet party. Simply make padded placemats as shown on page 68 and sew on plain coloured loops to contain knife, fork, dessert spoon, teaspoon and napkin.

We used a selection of pastels to create this multi-coloured setting, but you could also choose a single colour theme. Green would look particularly refreshing given the outdoor surroundings, blue is tranquil, pink pretty and yellow adds a welcome dash of brightness on a dull day. A plain PVC cloth emphasizes any of these colours, but you might also select a PVC version of the cotton used for placemats and use the same design to line the hamper. Cushions in the same print offset by plain rugs and parasols would give a fully co-ordinated effect. Toughened glass tableware adds a translucent air and is a sensible choice if you don't want to risk your best china. Unlike earthen-ware, it is light to carry and unlikely to chip, combining the advantages of china with the practicality of plastic.

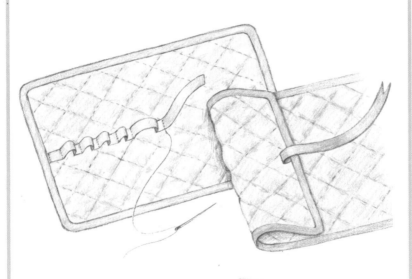

Placemats with ribbon loops make a pretty and practical container for cutlery and napkins. Use ribbon or tape at least 12 mm (¹/2 in) wide, experimenting with your own cutlery and rolled napkins to make loops of the right size. A single ribbon 30 cm (12 in) long is needed.

SOME LIKE IT HOT

There's nothing nicer than eating out of doors on a still summer night with the scent of flowers mingling with that of the charcoal grill. If you provide the setting for an impromptu party, chances are friends will chip in with sausages, steak and robust red wine. You don't even need a huge garden. A tiny patio or balcony will do, as long as you dress the table with vibrant colour and find enough dishes and chairs. Provide adequate lighting, too, with tree lights, garden flares or outdoor candles, to illuminate the cooking and serving areas.

A scheme full of strong contrasts can be exciting and will help to put your guests in party mood. We've used a white garden table, but you could improvise by covering

an ordinary table, or even an old door, with a brightly coloured paper or PVC cloth or sparkling white sheet. Disposable tableware in hot, zingy primary colours saves you the trouble of washing up and the possibility of breakages. Use paper cups to hold plastic cutlery for the children, with proper knives and forks on racks for adults. Have masses of extra napkins, as many people end up eating with their fingers. Add more colour to the table with lots of bright flowers. Green salads, gleaming fruits, creamy dips and hunks of warm bread look inviting and will supplement the meatier fare. Warm red wine near the barbecue; chill the white in pots of iced water.

Children can enjoy a lunchtime barbecue too; but when the sun is hot and high everyone needs cooling non-alcoholic drinks. A parasol or two will be important to give shade, and the colour scheme should be cool: ice-cream tones of pistachio and pink or a refreshing aquamarine.

PERFECT PARTNERS

A cheese and wine party can be an elegant, as well as an easy way to entertain. It offers the opportunity to try a new wine or a different cheese or dip — and gives you the chance to present them in your very own style.

Arrangement is all-important, but with such a variety of food, there's no need for a complicated centrepiece. In the candlelight this bowl of fruit looks almost like a still life. Studded with blossoms, it is as effective as a purely floral arrangement. We went to the expense of buying a length of marbled fabric in soft green and white to turn into a table-cloth and napkins. It's surprising how few people think to make table linen though it's a simple and inexpensive way to co-ordinate a room. The marble slab on which

the cheeses and water biscuits are arranged repeats the pattern and plays a practical role in keeping the cheese cool. Make your own labels for the different cheeses and choose with care. Strong cheese like Dolcelatte will give off a faint aroma of ammonia unless kept cool.

For a different style of presentation choose cheeses and wines from a specific country and dress the table to suit. For a Gallic atmosphere set Brie, Camembert and a variety of delicious soft cheeses on a table covered in a red and white check cloth with onions and garlic strung behind the table as a backdrop. If you want to emphasize wine rather than cheese take those from a particular region: Californian wines could set the scene for a Hollywood style party for example. Don't be afraid to do something out of the ordinary. Your table setting can help to break the ice and provide a talking point, not only on the day of the party but for many days to come.

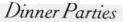
Dinner Parties

TO THE MANNER BORN

Sparkling crystal, glittering silver, fine bone china and Venetian candles are the hallmarks of the formal dinner party, whether it's held to celebrate a birthday or anniversary, to entertain colleagues or simply to enjoy a meal with friends. And if you and your guests have gone to the bother of dressing for it, why not ensure that the table is decorated in similar style? Trail ivy and silk roses down the centre and place tiny rosebuds at the corner of each napkin to complement the centrepiece and the design of the fine bone china.

Formal occasions don't demand grand, contrived flower arrangements. Simplicity is often the best policy, for the aim is to provide a welcoming atmosphere for your guests, and it's more important to relax them than to impress them. Flowers invite them to come closer so dress the living room as well as the dining table — the mantlepiece is a particularly effective place to put flowers. Do make sure that flowers on the table are kept low — about 30cm (1 ft) high — so that guests don't have to peer round them. Use a round centrepiece for a round table and an oblong one for a rectangular design. Flowers should be in keeping with your china, cloth and napkins, and emphasize their effect by your choice of candles.

Venetian candles are classics, plain, smooth and tapered. They burn slowly and are perfect for large table centres. The tall, delicate candles called flower lights look pretty in fine candle holders or massed in modern candelabra. Chunky or round candles are stable and burn for the longest time. Whichever type you choose, make sure that they are securely positioned to avoid accidents. Classic candles call for traditional candlesticks or candelabra, slender candles need candle holders to suit. Wide-based candles can be placed in a shallow holder or a saucer, which is easily hidden with flowers and greenery. Improvise by using florist's foam, plasticine or even a spiked meat platter, but make sure that the holder can support the weight of the candle and that the arrangement is not top-heavy or liable to fall. The same advice applies to the flower arrangement. If you want to copy this idea for a trailing centrepiece using fake ivy, secure it firmly to the candelabra as nothing is worse than a decoration that falls to pieces. Attention to detail is necessary at a formal dinner party — polish the glass till it gleams, shine the cutlery, and starch and iron the table linen. Finally, make sure that your guests know where they are sitting, to save embarrassment as they shuffle round the table.

SWISH 'N' CHIC

A modern table setting for a dinner party calls for striking colours. Here we used black with dashes of vivid yellow, emphasized by the tulips and slices of lemon floating in the finger bowls. Keep the table quite graphic; the tulips help here because they make such marvellous shapes as they bend.

The modern style should be simple, so choose plain china like this, where the only concession to pattern is the fine grey stripe. To add interest, alternate the colours of the napkins (we made these from remnants of fabric) and choose colours to blend with your dining table and china. Tie up with contrasting ribbon and use cutlery with coloured handles. You can vary the colours by using shocking pink and black with a pink flower head in place of lemon in the finger bowls and bright pink tulips, or choose black and red, which always looks dramatic. Keep the glasses simple and opt for those with a beautiful shape, making the whole setting very elegant and stylish.

Using
LIGHTING

Candles and Candlesticks

Candles are more useful for decoration than for the flattering light they give. Do not rely on them to give enough light for carving, serving hot soup or pouring drinks unless you are willing to use them in lavish quantities.

Left to right: Tall candles create interest when they are at different heights, either because you have burned them for varying lengths of time or use holders of different sizes (though the same design and colour). Nightlights cast a friendly glow. Use them around the room as well as on the table. Grand candelabra are, by contrast, formal and impressive, calling for slender tapers. Flower rings are easy to make from cubes of florist's foam, candles inserted in the top with fresh blooms and foliage hiding the base.

They are particularly useful when children are present, as they cannot be knocked over without going out. Always put them in a saucer — or pretty bowl — of water.

Light Fittings

Lighting serves two main purposes, to create atmosphere and to allow you to serve and eat in comfort. If used with supplementary lights, such as wall lamps or a freestanding uplighter, a pendant lamp centred over the dining table fulfils this function well, throwing an inviting pool of light. A rise-and-fall mechanism allows the light to hang low during the meal and to be raised clear afterwards

Use downlights to emphasize an arrangement of flowers or other centrepiece. Projecting from the ceiling, they throw a narrow beam of light which, while drawing attention to one object, still gives plenty of light for diners to eat in comfort. They can also be recessed into the ceiling, where the effect is much more subtle. In this case you would need to use several to cast an even light. Downlights give a pleasant light that is still even and bright enough to work in.

A single central light is undesirable because it casts a flat light that can make your guests feel uncomfortably under examination. Where there is no space for anything but ceiling lights, lights hanging at different levels provide an unusual answer. Ceiling roses that hold more than one flex and special hooks to fix the flexes wherever you want are available. Used with dimmer switches, lights at varying levels can be very versatile.

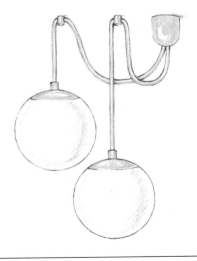

A Fine Romance

Saint Valentine's Day is the traditional time to stage a romantic dinner for two, but any excuse will do! Use a small round or square table, such as a card table, for intimacy and set two places facing each other. Then see what space you have left for decoration. The table setting should be soft and delicate, with candles to cast a flattering light. If you want to eat outdoors substitute a candle in a storm lantern or glass container. A gentle, two-colour scheme is ideal. White lace laid over a pink or blue cloth creates a background for pastel and white china and the theme may be extended to the centrepiece. Here a posy of full-blown roses is kept low so that it doesn't obstruct lingering glances, while candles add height. A round arrangement was chosen to reflect the shape of the table and even the food was selected to blend with the scheme —

white bread with tiny whorls of smoked salmon, prawn cocktails, and glasses of rosé wine or pink champagne.

The background can be a plain pink sheet or piece of fabric. Tie pale pink ribbon in bows through the lace top cloth and decorate the pretty pink napkins with a flower. Cutlery, china and glass should harmonize with the delicate effect; long-stemmed glasses and tall candles make good partners, while the pink and white dishes blend with the colour scheme. Both the table setting and the meal should be planned so that you can concentrate on your guest. A cold first course and pudding are practical and can be pretty too if you choose colours to match the setting. You might choose raspberry sorbet to end this meal for instance, and you could extend the theme to the main course by serving salmon or lobster. Put candles in the freezer while you are cooking the meal. If they are cold and hard they will not drip when alight. Place a mirror where it will reflect the scene to double its effect and make sure that the table looks pretty from every angle.

ORIENTAL IMPRESSION

The art of the Orient relies on simplicity and shape, as much as pattern, for effect. To recreate this atmosphere further west, use low furniture backed by a screen made from three hinged panels covered with tracing paper. You could use a coffee table to eat at and seat your guests on cushions, but here we have chosen a special low table with matching chairs for greater comfort.

Black, red and white make a strong statement. As the table is low, the single blooms upon it have been chosen so that they have just as much impact when looked on from above. As an alternative, a single twig could be taken from the garden, sprayed black and decorated with narrow knots of ribbon. It should have an interesting asymmetrical shape for the correct oriental effect. In place of napkins, there are red flannels tied with thin black ribbon. They should be warm, damp, and scented (wring them out in

hot water and sprinkle with lemon) to wipe away grease, as some Chinese food is eaten with the fingers. Decorate the table with concertina fans sprayed black, but use cheap flat oriental fans as placemats, painted black to match the decor. They can be given to your guests to take home as a souvenir of the meal.

Flat and shallow items evoke the art of the Orient. Use bamboo mats in place of fans if you prefer and translucent porcelain bowls. Lay chopsticks by all means, but play safe by putting forks ready for those who aren't adept at the skill of oriental eating.

Look east for inspiration when planning the table setting. Ikebana turns flower arranging into an art form, exercising great restraint in the choice of materials. Twigs play an important part for Ikebana has a philosophical as well as an aesthetic aim — to attain consummate beauty by using the minimum amount of plants. In keeping with this approach, scatter flower petals over the table in a colour to suit your scheme or float single flower heads in shallow dishes filled with water.

THE RAJ DUET

As more people learn to appreciate Indian cooking, so it
warrants an appropriately stylish setting. Ornaments
from the Far East are inexpensive and widely available, so
select table accessories in rich warm colours or embel-
lished with gold or brass, with joss sticks to scent the air.
Make the atmosphere ornate but welcoming, using an
Indian bedspread as a tablecloth partnered by another
which acts as a backcloth on the wall behind. Put out
gleaming brass vases for decoration; serve water in huge
carafes clinking with ice with lager and cider in pewter
beakers to add to the emphasis on precious metals. China
in rich russet and blue with gold edging, the dishes resting
on brass trays continues the theme. Brass bangles or
curtain rings can replace napkin rings, and candles in a
deep rich red are set in brass holders. Spray leaves or

wicker baskets gold to give them an expensive gleam and use fine gold wrapping paper to line dishes and trays. Dark orange paper napkins add warmth and provide extra colour.

Copper, silver, pewter and brass are splendid foils for plants of all kinds. Here we used a single spray of exotic flowers and leaves placed at the back of the table rather than at the centre which would interfere with sampling food from the different dishes involved.

For food, consider pilau rice garnished with fruit and almonds, meat spiced and marinated in yoghurt before being crisped in the oven or chicken cooked with delicate spices such as cardamon. Side dishes should include papadoms and minty dips made with yoghurt, cucumber and a little garlic to cool the palate. Take the meal slowly, keeping the food warm on a beautiful brass heater with two long-lasting night lights underneath. Moody lighting makes the metal sparkle without overwhelming the food which, after all, is the jewel in your crown . . .

ACKNOWLEDGMENTS

The author and publishers would like to thank the following individuals and companies for their contribution to this book:

photograph on pages 6-7 by James Jackson, stylist Kit Johnson; jacket and all other photography by Malcolm Robertson; illustrations by Lucy Su.

for supplying wine: John Milroy Limited

for baking the traditional sheaf-of-wheat loaf on page 50: Albert Weaver, Master Baker, Wethersfield, Braintree, Essex

for the loan of the top hat and gloves on page 23: Moss Bros

for supplying merchandise for photography:

ribbons by Offray

silk flowers throughout from Sia U.K. Limited

pp. 6-7: china by Thomas, glasses by Dartington, cutlery and cruet from David Mellor; china, 'Countryware' by Coalport and 'Heritage' by Johnson; candleholders by Wedgwood; crystal glasses and cutlery from Dickins and Jones.
p. 16: china, 'Davenport' from Perrings; cutlery by Viners; glasses, 'Da Vinci' by Corning.
p. 17: damask cloth from Liberty; cutlery, 'Musketeer' by Dexam.
p. 18: china by Wedgwood from David Mellor; cutlery by Viners.
p. 19: cutlery by David Mellor; table-cloth and napkins from Liberty.

pp. 22-23: china from the Reject China Shop; champagne *flûtes*, 'Illusion' by Orrefors from Dexam; cutlery from Dexam; sweet dish from David Mellor.
pp. 28-29: china, 'April' by Coalport from Wedgwood Rooms; table-cloth and napkins from Liberty; champagne *flûtes*, 'Illusion' by Orrefors from Dexam.
pp. 32-33: china, 'Amherst' by Wedgwood; bowl by Orrefors, glasses and decanter, 'Susanne' from Dexam; cutlery by Viners; cruet from Thomas Goode.
pp. 34-35: table-cloth and napkins from Liberty; cocktail glasses from David Mellor; cocktail shaker by Viners; paper parasols from Marks and Spencer.
pp. 40-41: Walt Disney figurines and badges by Coalport from Wedgwood Rooms; pottery balloons from Sia.
pp. 46-47: china, 'Harmony' by Arzberg; napkins from Liberty.
pp. 50-51: glasses by Denby; lace napkins and pewter goblets from Liberty; all other items from David Mellor.
p. 52: glass bowl, jug and tumblers and star-shaped biscuit cutters from David Mellor; forks by Viners.
p. 53: glass punch bowl with ladle and cups from Liberty; cutlery by Viners.
pp. 54-55: china, 'Vieux Paris' by Haviland from the Reject China Shop; glass, 'Da Vinci' by Corning; napkins and lace curtains from Liberty; cutlery, 'Musketeer' by Dexam.

pp. 60-61: glasses by Orrefors from Dexam; sweet dish from David Mellor; crystal dish with silver rim by Orrefors; small presents and Christmas decorations from Marks and Spencer; table from Ulferts of Sweden.

pp. 62-63: china, 'Narumi Rouge' from the Reject China Shop; glasses by Denby.

pp. 64-65: china, 'Green Line' by Arzberg from the Reject China Shop; cutlery from Perrings; glass, Chinese side plates and oyster dishes from David Mellor.

p. 67: china, 'Schevenigen' by Thomas from the Reject China Shop; cutlery by Viners.

p. 71: china, 'Lemon Festival' by Arzberg; glasses by Denby; decanter by Dexam: cut glass vases from Marks and Spencer; cutlery by David Mellor; print from Perrings.

p. 72: coffee pot, cups and saucers 'Turquoise TCA' by Herend from Thomas Goode; table-cloth from Liberty.

p. 73: tea set, 'Apple Blossom' by Wedgwood; cutlery by Viners.

pp. 74-75: glass plates, 'Grape' by Boda from Dexam; cutlery by Viners; blanket and linens from Liberty; glasses, ice buckets and wine coolers from Marks and Spencer.

pp. 78-79: 'Lotus' bowls, red 'Arabia' bowls and cruet from David Mellor; cutlery on stand by Viners; plastic cutlery from Marks and Spencer.

pp. 80-81: white jug from Liberty; glasses by David Mellor; bowl on stand by Orrefors from Dexam.

pp. 82-83: china, 'Osborne' by Wedgwood; glasses 'Da Vinci' by Corning; napkins and placemats from Liberty; candelabra, cruet, decanters and tureen from Thomas Goode; dining table from Finewood Furniture.

p. 85: china, 'Toki' and glasses from Habitat; cutlery from David Mellor.

pp. 88-89: china, 'Kristina' from Habitat; glass dishes from David Mellor; cut glass bowl from Marks and Spencer; table linen from Liberty; cutlery and cruet by Viners.

pp. 90-91: black basalt bowl by Wedgwood from David Mellor; fans, mat and wicker serving dish from Liberty; flannels from Marks and Spencer; screen, 'Shoji' and table and chair, 'Gaijin' from the Futon Company.

pp. 92-93: glasses and jug, 'Helena' by Orrefors from Dexam; cotton bedspread, dishes, pewter and brassware and all other items from Liberty.

The Author's special thanks go to Linda Bamford, Linda Gray and Charles Shirvell.

USEFUL ADDRESSES

Corning Limited, Wear Glassworks, Sunderland

David Mellor, 4 Sloane Street, London SW1 and branches

Dexam International, Haslemere, Surrey

Dryad, P.O. Box 38, Northgates, Leicester LE1 9BU (for enamel paints by mail order)

Finewood Furniture, Seaford, Sussex

Futon Company, 82-83 Tottenham Court Road, London W.1

John Milroy Limited, 3 Greek Street, London W.1

Liberty & Co, 210-220 Regent Street, London W.1

London Wedding Company, 52 High Street, Acton, London W3 6LE

Moss Bros, Covent Garden, London W.C.2

Reject China Shop, Beauchamp Place, London W.1. and branches

Sia U.K. Limited, Parkside House, Grinstead Road, New Cross, London S.E.4

Thomas Goode & Co (London) Limited, 19 South Audley Street, Grosvenor Square, London W.1

Viners Cutlery, Trafalgar House, Edgware Road, London NW9 5EB

Wedding Bureau, 214 Evelyn Street, Deptford, London SE8 5BZ

INDEX